THE THINGS I NEVER SAID

The Things I Never Said

K.L. Neal

Copyright © 2023 by K.L. Neal

All rights reserved.

No portion of this book may be reproduced in any form without written permission from the publisher or author, except as permitted by U.S. copyright law.

Hold on, darling, even if the light grows dim

When I think of sixteen
I still think of it as who I was supposed to be
There's two parallels
The first of the reality
The second of the fantasy
In it, I don't think of the sadness
The way I sat at my desk, drowning alive
Afire in my mind
Warmed by the burning of the last of my dreams
No, I think of the time; I think of the place
Where I stood in the mirror
Realizing that I no longer looked the same
What clothes still fit had taken a new shape
The hugged me where I had changed
And I hated it
The way I looked
The way I felt
The way people looked at me
I went from a girl, strong and resilient
To jagged pieces of who I had been
Unable to function but as half of who I am
And somedays I still look in the mirror
And the only reflection is the girl
Who stopped loving herself when she turned sixteen

Of all the things I never said
Of all the confessions unuttered
Left rattling like empty bowls
In the cupboard in my head
Of all the things I've regretted to believe
And, shamefully, I admit, believed to regret
Of all the things I never showed
And now will never know
I'm afraid I have more regrets than satisfaction
In the life I've led
However, I must tell you that of all my blunders,
My faults, and my failures
So many things terrify me
But the most that frightens me
Is I never told him
That he was the nicest man I'd ever met

I want to be light
Unburdened by gravity
Like the fall breeze
But I'm afraid

Hear me, darling
When I tell you that
It's not bad to go through seasons
Does not the very cusp of this world do the same?
As warm as it is
It cannot be summer forever
Not here
Not yet
Some time
Soon
But just not yet

I feel rotten for feeling old in my youth of twenty-two
But when they've been years spent alone
With few friends and less suitors
Dare I say, I've always felt a little like a loser
I was twenty-one before I went on a date
And I had to sit on my hands for the way
The years of anticipation made them shake
Because I was terrified
Just driving around that little town in his car
Feeling like he was judging me
Measuring
Weighing me
As if we both knew, I wasn't enough to fit
Into his world of pretty, perfect things

So much I regret believing but feared to ever show
In protection of myself
And now, I'll never know
If I had said something different
Said something more right
If that would put the excitement
Back into the hope in my life
If I had said something else
Something more clever or funny
I will never know if that—
Would that have made any difference
In where we stand now
Across the world's excuse of circumstance
That we're too different or the timing's not right
There was *something* in his eyes
In the way he looked at me on that dark winter night
Right?
Like he thought or saw
Something
Some glimpse that said volumes
Of whom I was or who we would be
And in the moment
I thought he was contemplating the possibility
Of how we came to be driving through town on a weeknight
Or how he could end things without rallying a fight

Hold on, darling, I know the light grows dim
The shadows draw down from the mountain's rim
What moonlight remains to guide you through the night
Is but enough to see you safe
But not enough to lead you home or let you inside
It is enough for the world you know
But not enough to take you where you could go
Just hold on, darling
I know the light grows dim

I'm afraid I'll crumble if I ever hear someone say,
I'll leave the light on for you
As I drive home
Through a cool fall night
To a place where I belong
Where the key slips easily
Into the lock on the front door
Which guards the house
Not to keep me out
But to keep me safe; for I am home
It protects the things I care about
For now, such a feeling exists only in my head
But somehow, someday, I hope to make it real

It's days like today
That make me wish
He gave it another try
I also wish I had fought harder
Been bolder
Faced his blue eyes
And asked why

My darling, the only way to reach the other side
Is to chase the light
You must work through what you avoid
Not for the sake of the work
But for the way it changes your soul
Day after heart wrenching
Obliterating day of pain
Scoop together the wobbly pieces
Of the broken clay
Add a little water
And with gentle hands
Love it back into itself
Until your heart and you remember what it means
To feel whole again

I never said that I nearly died at sixteen
I don't mean physically
Please don't worry
I mean mentally, emotionally—spiritually
I took a hammer to something
Inside me that once ticked
I beat it and beat it until I stopped it
From ever driving me forward again
To keep from falling from the pedestal
I chained myself to the bottom of the well
That I drowned in
I stayed so long under the waters
That when I surfaced from the top of the dark places I'd been
All of me filled my lungs with water
But so distraught for oxygen
I couldn't tell sea from land
I just drank whatever I could find
Until my equilibrium broke
While the world still spun
And I just sat in the bottom of my shower
Grasping at water
Thinking it was air

Forgive me for talking so long
To pensively ask for your forgiveness
I mistreated your memory
As if it were not my own blood and flesh
That made me the woman wired to run
And when I tried to stop running
I think I tried to play God
And become the maker of my own destiny
What was I supposed to do
With his pretty hair and eyes so blue
How could I not think
At last! I have found someone who looks like me
·But his soul and mine were not compatible
We weren't even birds of a feather
I let him hurt you
Because I thought he would see how great you are
He would fight the monsters, rescue the girl
Right the wrongs
That I committed to you when I whispered
That I wasn't enough
I think you knew
You were half the whisper in my chest
That made me restless when me and him talked
From the inside, you saw the struggle
Of me stuffing him into my box
Forgive me for trying to force the idea
Of someone who doesn't know you like I do
To love you and fix the ways I broke you

- *dear sixteen-year-old me*

I never said that I doubt every day
If a love as powerful as the sea
Is meant for a freckle-face, misshapen
Woman like me
How could the God
Who made something as perfect as a butterfly
Make a caterpillar like me
And leave me without metamorphosis
Just this round little thing
Inching along the ground
Watching everyone else hatch from their shell
And soar
The way I thought life would be for me
I didn't expect to hurt so much
Watching people lead the life
I thought was meant for me

The funny thing about all the things
The vastness of everything that I never told him
I don't know if I could still find the words
If he stood in front of me
It's like I only know how to talk to his memory

It doesn't matter how many calories I cut
How many I add
My body stays the same
Buried by the pounds
Short-statured
Round featured
With a slightly crooked nose
It doesn't matter if I throw myself through a workout
Day after day
It doesn't matter if I add more rest days
I stay the same
It feels like I'm trapped in my skin
Like the person I am is disconnected
From whom I look like I am
And I can't decide which is worse
That it consumes my thoughts
Or that I let it cripple me

You are born of tenacity and fire,
I tell myself in the mirror
But I don't believe it
They're just words to make me think
I'm anything more than what I really am
Which explains why I'm always surprised
At the way I watch the sky change
And catch myself still marveling
At the wonder
That it changes every day
Yet I still stop and stare—every time
And I wonder if I can be like that

When I think of you
I think of coffee
And that's a first for me
I never drink the stuff
If I do, it's a novelty
I usually prefer tea
...yet with you
Oh, what have I let you make me become!
For the first time in my life
I don't know which direction to run
To stay means to let myself slowly grow
To be fully known
Something of which I let few see
But it also means I'm exposed
To the impression of what you think of me
What you'd have me be
Where worlds collide
Was where your soul meant mine
I don't think we were meant for anything
More than just passing as continental drifts
As grating tectonic plates marring the other
So now we pretend not to see each other on the sidewalk
But turn to look back after we pass

Someone should have warned me about reading old texts
And if someone did
Please, you should have warned me again
I'm driving myself mad, rereading what he said to me
I found an old message from the weekend after our first date
I had told a friend that you were likely disappointed
After going out with me
Because we were so different
Having to adapt our plans
Change our schedules
Just to go for a walk
My friend read all that and wrote me back, *He wasn't*
Seeing that text made me want to laugh and cry
Like I read it again for the first time

Could growing up come with a guidebook
Like, could my older self write back to who I was
The girl who made the woman in me
Could I write to her to tell her
Don't worry about fourteen
It'll be the best year of your life
You'll play volleyball everyday
And learn how you love to write stories
Your clothes will fit
You'll feel comfortable in your skin
And at fifteen, you'll stop playing
Not for a loss of the love of the game
It just won't be the same
People will make it that way
And at sixteen, you'll crumble
No, you'll shatter
You'll rebuild a little
Then, you'll crumble at seventeen
By eighteen, you'll be so tired of holding it all together
That you'll give up on decisions
And let others live for you
At nineteen, you'll be exhausted
At twenty, you'll be alone
At twenty-one, you'll be heart broken
And it'll be by your own hand
And into your twenties and into the world
You'll go without a plan
But along the way
You'll meet so many people
And see so many scenes
Wonders beyond your wildest dreams
And you will learn that nothing lasts forever
Not the good and not the bad
Life is full of seasons

And there is nothing to do but keep living
And love the one you're in
If it's possible
Could somebody tell that to me
When I was fourteen

While I don't think we'll grow old together
Today, I want your hand to hold
But that's not fair to want you today
Knowing we won't last till tomorrow

There're days where I think I'm alright
There're days I forget any pain from you ever happened
Except then I go to a coffee shop
And I catch myself looking at every face at every table
Wondering if I'll see you there
If you'll be deep in your studies
Pouring over notes at a table or in a chair
Along the wall or corner of the room
I scour the places
That I go alone
Because I'm hoping then I'll have an excuse
To spend the day, the afternoon, just a moment
Talking to you

A forest can become a swamp
And the mule deer knows how to swim
But that doesn't make it a fish
No more than drowning a forest makes it a marsh
If you want me, I'll be whatever you need
I can't tell you how to love
But I don't want you to be on a mission to change me
Love me, wild, or let me be

Driving in your car
I sat so small in my seat
Safety laying at my feet
Like a blanket across my legs
Comforting me that you'd never hurt me
In any time or any place
Never intentionally
It eased me back into the chair
Relaxing the stiffness of my form
Like I could still clutch my guard
To my chest
Less in fear and more like
How a child sleeps with a bear
Not cowering under the covers
But gently going into the next
The headlights lighting the way
A turn, then another
A sigh, and I drew a deep breath

Funny, darling, how we met at night
But I live with your memory in a daydream

I'd like to say I'm sorry
You saw the personality that comes out
To protect who I am
How was I to know if you would see me
And savor the forest
Or if you would see the thorns and the brambles?
I send many scrambling for the nearest tower
High above the thicket that snags at your skin
Like the thorned claws of a monster
When really, they're just trying to protect the flowers
And the wild things that grow within

And the heartache and the pain
Drive me back to the paper
Like the river rises to the rain

Maybe all I really need is someone to listen
Maybe that's why I force words onto people
Try to explain their emotions before they can
To prove my intelligence
That I understand
It distracts me from what I am
And what I'm not
It hides the insecurity I wear beneath boxy clothes
And address my insecurity first thing
When I walk in a room
Because I want everyone else to know that I know
That I look bad
So no one feels the need to tell me
That I look awful
That I should brush my hair
That I should find some cream
To balance the rosacea
That I should see what the girl next to me does
And try to imitate her because
She's better than I'll ever be
Yet, in striving, maybe somehow
The ugly parts of me
Will cease to be
And I will become something better
More like her, less like me
I've yet to find a way to walk into a room
And say, *Hello, everyone, this is me*

You have no idea how much I could have loved you

I lay awake and wonder if he heard
About me from any of his friends
Did they give advice through the weekend
Or did they ever know
I understand if he never told them
I understand if he sought their advice
Even though it doesn't change the way it ended
This dying ember-light
In me still wants to know

I wish I could have seen you grin at me
Like that
But maybe not
This way is for the best

If I said all the things in my mind
I know I'd never let your hand go
I'd endure endlessly
Because I don't think I'll ever run out of things I could say
I don't know if I'll ever be able to fully convey
The thin grasp of my understanding of what we were
As I pour from myself until I'm wrung dry
Sucking the dew from the morning like the desert
Dried to the earth 'til it cracks through the crust
And though I've cried over you no more than twice
It's like the salt bridge has corroded the connection
From the longing in my heart
To the logic in my mind

I say I could have loved you
Yet in the name of full confession
I'm afraid I'd have taken you to change you
That's what I would have done with you
Washed the concrete from your suburbs
Planted you in the life of my make-believe
In the forest, of the trees, changing, I'm afraid
I'd have made you
To be less like you and more like me

I'm of the forest, drawn to the rocks and mountains
If the stars are not your lamplight
If the river does not make you draw deeper breath
If you were not willing to climb great depths
To see the lowest of my soul
Why did I expect you to stay
When you were born of a different way

When I said it was okay
Repeated it twelve times
Told you that it was alright
That I'd be just fine
I said it at first
Because I didn't know what to say
The second came out like a half-muttered praise
Because I didn't have to decide how I felt anymore
If I liked the idea of you because you looked like home
Or were just the sight of land to a wayfaring sailor
Months from seeing the shore
But what I really meant
So suppressed in my body that I didn't even hear
The whisper in my head
Except for a faint stirring
Like the wind rising or the trees moaning
Because I recognized the way that your eyes
Started to avoid mine
And how you kept apologizing without saying anything
Vocalizing that you didn't wish to do this
And understood how unfortunate it is
To have such a conversation
Especially in a public place
Like you could somehow spare me from the open disgrace
What I never had the chance to tell you was that
I've gotten pretty good at masking my emotions
Oh, sure I still wear them on my face and on my sleeve
And everyone gets the notion that they think they know
What I'm thinking
And often times they're right
But there are several occasions
Sometimes in more than one evening
Where I feel like crying but can successfully hide
In my room or behind a mask

Like steaming fog conceals the glass
In the shower where I want to cry
So all you can see is the outline
Of a woman humming a lullaby
And while the lullaby comforts you that I'll be alright
It really is a woman trying to tell herself that it's okay
If she cries herself to sleep that night
Cause the hope hurts more than anything I've come to realize
The hope pushes me to take a leap
It doesn't matter how immersive the height
Whether it's a mountain or less than two feet
And though I hesitant
I jump
And sink to the bottom every time
But when I was younger
I didn't know I could be strong enough to leap and dive
So there's that at the least
To comfort me when I cry

It's been a really good day
And all I want to do is tell you all about it

Do you know how many days I just waste away
Because I know that if I try nothing
I can never fail
And while it eats at me
Subconsciously
I've come to think
That it's better to do what will result
With things I know
Rather than risk even a fraction
I am my own captive

A small part of me is always worried
That I could change my entire self
And no one would ever see
That I was no longer me

How do you sever a relationship
After spending so many hours talking in a day
Perhaps the same way
I've kept the romantics as platonic—
Turn off the emotion
Grow numb to everything
Dismiss it all in one motion

How was I supposed to know what to say
When he asked me about the hard things in life
How I was supposed to look into his blue eyes and tell him
That I stare in the mirror and compare my body
At twenty-two
To when I was fourteen

Whose fault is it that you couldn't stay platonic
You know I am unbridled
A runner, a chaser, a dreamer
You know I build my imagination
To produce the wildest of simple fantasies
A little home, a little land,
Bold ambitions and ghosts of abandoned fruitions
And none of them ever involved you
So don't blame your tears on me
I wasn't the one who tried to change things
Bit much?
That's what you're getting into with me

When you first saw the green flecks in my eyes
Did you ever think you'd end up crying over me

A pensive thinker, someone kind
I figured that out
When his eyes pierced mine like a heartbreak
When he said he'd pay for my drink
When he opened every door
Like he couldn't believe that
I didn't know I deserved to be treated that way
To let someone take care of me
Even with the utmost of little things

It's been one of those days
Where I'm left so cracked
It takes every ounce of my self-respect
And determination not to call
And ask you to hold me

There were little things I learned
From a relationship that ended
Before he rounded the last bend
To take me back to my home
I learned that I like little things
Like someone grabbing extra napkins
Or following me around
To my side of the car
To open the door for me
Whether my hands were full or not
I learned that I still miss
Texts in the morning
If I won't see him all day
I liked supporting him
Even just by asking about his game
That I couldn't make
I liked the way he looked at my eyes
And the way the moon softened his
As we drove through the city
On cool wintry nights
He taught me in a relationship
What it meant to be kind

He has no idea how forever special
I hold September
Please don't read that and feel a burden
I don't blame him
He didn't take away
He gave me something to have
A memory
No matter how far time stretches
It's a memory all mine
One I remember with the utmost of gratitude
For I can genuinely say
I've never met someone like him
Someone who set my standards so high
Higher than I thought possible to dream

Oh, I've let you run away with my mind
Taking my hand in my dreams
Like I wish you really had with mine

Forgive me for the way I looked at you
Like I wished you were someone else
Though you should know
That you're wonderful
That's another thing I never said
I should have said so many things
Even though I knew we weren't made for rings

It takes the weight of the strain
From the sound of your name
When someone asks how we are
And I have to bear the bad news
That there's no one like you
Yet you made the decision
To put back the division
That separates you from my friend
Who is a boy from something with a deeper end
It's not something I like to readily admit
Yet there's no fruition in throwing a fit
Because we're past the point of no return
.Hear the echo of the gavel to call this meeting adjourned
But still, I refuse to let go
Of the places we could have gone
Of the people we could have become
And I would do it all over again
Even if I could've foreseen the end for you and me

Someone to take care of me
Someone to take care of
Found in the same person
Oh, what bliss
Could such mystics exist

No matter the years, the laughs, the hikes, the sunrises
A mirror will always make me say
Am I pretty enough to convince you to stay
Or is the moment coming when I'll have to
Watch you walk away

I've decided to thank God in the morning
For another day
For the way the birds sing
The way the trees in the wind sway
It's nothing of my work
It doesn't belong to me
Yet I feel it as part of me
As if my soul yearns for the mountains
Because it knows it was meant to soar
Through the great heights
I've decided to thank the people who listen the most
Who take my boastful professions
And my whispered transgressions
And then level my voice
Until my strivings turn from ache to rest

You treated me better than right
You were more; you were kind
I'll always regret not asking why you smiled
At me like that
When you heard the heavy honey in my accent
It's an eclipse that sticks to me
But instead of scrubbing it with hate
I'll thank the experience for what it gave
Never did I ever think I'd learn so much of myself
From one person
As it seems that though we were not made for each other
We were meant to meet each other

How do I feel? I'm not sure
How do I tell if it's love or if I'm bored
All I know is that
I'm out of words to say besides
I miss you

I'd have liked to go to a museum with him
Walk from room to room
Looking at the ancient things
Of people who were and used to be
As part of the world as him and me

Oh, my goodness, if you could have seen the chaos that ensued
When I was getting ready for my first date with him
You would laugh if you knew the way my roommates fussed
Over my hair and my preplanned order and the way I dressed
Pink sweatshirt to bring out the color in my eyes
Then just a casual pair of jeans and tennis shoes to hide
How nervous I was to be appraised by him
And of course, I have no clue what to do
When I like a boy, and I never mentioned
I really wanted to be pretty enough to keep your attention
My hair curled in long, loose waves
That cascaded down my back and framed my face
A final touch, and I was ready to go
Sitting with my shoes and keys by the phone
And as he had said, right on the dot
He called that he was outside at eight o'clock
I said through the apartment, *He's calling me*
And my roommates shouted from my room
With the utmost glee
From my room where they waited with my blinds cracked
To watch me leave in the night painted black
Then their well wishes were drowned by the sound
Of their cheers when, from his side, he came around
And opened my door to get in the car
And they jumped so hard
They knocked my curtains twice from the wall
I don't remember many of the details
A surprise for me, from one who loves to be precise
But still, I remember a hundred million little things
He shut the door and walked through the headlights
As I stared over the dash at the wonder of the night
Sending me further into the questions
Of how I had managed to sneak past social normalcy
For who knows the story where

The plain, freckled-like-a-pockmark girl
Gets the good guy, easy on the eyes
With something of a depth to his soul
That's never how it goes
Yet there I sat in the passenger's seat
As he got in and drove off, right next to me
And I cannot tell you a single word that I said
I just remember looking straight ahead, out of the way
Because it was all so new
The night, the date, sitting there
The way I felt him stare

This started off as a way
To understand why
No, it was something more than that
Like a last dying sigh
As I picked up the broken pot
Of what I planted
Hoping that by the spring
I could be enchanted
With the flowers that bloom
On this little breath of life
And let the yellow colors
That I decided to add into my life
Make me smile in the morning
And let the leaves dance with the fading memory
Golden in my mind in all its glory

It wasn't him
It was the feeling of being pursued
That felt like a blanket
Heavy on my chest
Letting me breathe easier
So when the feeling was gone
I found myself missing
Not him but the feeling

There are lots of things I never said
I'm no different than the rest
Nothing special
Nothing unique
I think I'm average in every way
With diminishing returns
On how interesting I am
Directly related to the length of time you know me
I fear I will bore someone
If any tried to be my friend
And if I actually found a good man
Oh, Heaven, forbid that he sees first the real me
He'd never stay

When I think of you in the morning
I do the opposite of soar
I sink into a muddle
A mess of thought
Emotions in puddles
Because when the sun touches a new day
I remember that I couldn't make you stay
All over again
Day after day

I need you like a plant needs a drink
In the most vehement of thunderstorms
There's no time to think
For the way the rain pours sideways
As I fly down the byways and highways
Everything is wind-torn into a shredded mess
Throwing leaves and debris
And when at last I'm home
I drop to my knees in the shower
And let the rain fall down my back
I don't have time to stop and let it soak in
To my skin and heal the love-parched cracks
I catch but a drop or two
As it all comes down
Throwing the thundering sounds
Round after round
Till it floods the places of all things green
From dust to drowned
And it soaks into the hem of my jeans
Like roots setting into the ground
Because I have no understanding of which way to go
Other than to weather the storm
And take the uncertainty with whichever
Way the wind blows
And so, this chaos that ensues me
That surrounds and consumes me
Leaves no want for water
But makes well known the absence of a long slow day
Waiting on another time when in the quiet of the night
I'll find someone who'll look at me that way
When I jump and find that hope didn't come with me
That the parachute it promised lays tucked
Still at the pilot's feet
That I'm free-falling in the consequences

Of mine own actions
And I've done it so often
It's like an old friend, my reaction
I do the same thing every time
I pick up a pen and decide if it's prose or rhyme
To try to sift through the muddle
And discern the potting soil from the mud that I've made
With tears of hope that fall like rain

I can't find a reason to hate you
The only reason I can find
Is that you looked at me and walked away
And I can't blame you for that
I can't
Because I've had my share aplenty
Of boys who made offers for my hand
But I don't know if I'd call any of them a man
Nothing more than chew toys in the jaws of a lion
Helpless, groveling at what's transpired
Spouting big attitudes and pride that will stagger
With them right out the door
Dripping in disgrace
Silent with the dejection written on their faces
There're not even the sounds of a sigh
As I let them leave their flowers to whither
On the cold ground
Outside my front door
Where the welcome mat is worn and torn
From my feet coming and going
Looking around and searching and knowing
That I may look for a lifetime and more
And I may never find anything more beautiful
Than the way I know your
Eyes will hold mine
In the dying starlight
Of a brilliant fall night

I never told him that I wanted to wear his hoodie
That I would have made him cookies
Made sure that after the games
And the long, hard days
I made food and had something for him to drink
I never said that I don't love halfway
I give it all
As I give it away
And more times than not
I'm drained so far
To the bottom of the barrel
That I cut the rough ends to scrape together
Some sense of emotion
To spoon feed myself the last drop of love
Except there always seems to be one person I missed
And the final tablespoon goes to their lips
To feed their hunger to be known a little more

I am like a book on a shelf in an old forgotten library
In the days of the past
Maybe some young heart would have seen my depth
Plucked me from the masses
To read the spine and admire the cover
Some may have read me once
Some maybe twice
But maybe, just maybe
Not for the print
Not for the cover
I was someone's favorite story

After we talked, I felt myself moving on
In bits and pieces at a time
Until the day that my words turned into a silly rhyme
And I found an outlet thinking that I could drain myself
Of this caustic hope that's eating my soul
From the inside to the ground
Till it buries me into the ashes of the bridges that I burned
By insisting I give every possible reason
For him to place me back on the shelf
My broken heart, full of waiting love, now scorned

It would've been nice to know if what I felt
Was just a fabrication in my head
Some twist of reality to fill the whole inside of me
And pass the time until I find
The one who can make me laugh
Or if it was something real
That we decided wasn't worth the effort to try

Give my grief a rest
Because I can't keep dancing
With your memory in my head
If I have to spin under your arm once more
There will be nothing left of me but a mess on the floor
I'm seeing stars
Counting them like I'm
Numbering the ways that I should have fought harder
To give you a reason to want to talk
Till you never ran out of questions
As we strolled the boardwalk

The Things I Never Said

I never told you that I prefer tea over coffee
All I said was that I dislike the brewed stuff
Unless it's freezing outside with ice or snow on the ground
And if I do drink it, I prefer it plain
Maybe with a little milk, a little honey
If I'm feeling fancy
I have my favorites
I frequent those selections like my habit
Of walking with you
Except when we do
It's in thought
Because you made it impossible to ever go do
Something like that, something like a walk
Something simple and delicate for the innocence of it
Something I treasure so ardently like it's dearly beloved
Because I can picture it, oh, so clearly in my head
As vivid as the conversation on the day we met
Because another thing I never said
Is that I began to plan another date the day before you left

Someday, though, I'll have to stop writing
And just get over you

My chest tightens when I look at my plate
It's been so long of measuring and weighing
Every gram
Of every ounce
That I can't decide if it's wrong or right
To keep going like this
Because if I stop
If I start to let go
I don't know what'll happen
But I'm already not what I want to be
So now I want to give up trying
But calories make my chest tight
Because they say, *Eat less*
Exercise more
But I did that
I tried that
I ate little until I ate less
And I exercised more
Until my feet dragged against the floor
As I walked across campus for class
Holding my hand to my stomach
Lecturing that I wasn't hungry
My body was wrong
This was the best way
After all, can't you see the bones on the stray
Isn't that the best way to see my collar bones again
I wish I could go back to twenty
And shake her
For thinking she didn't need to eat
That she would endure
Until she looked better than the best
Oh, what folly did I accept as truth
I'd rather stay the same than try that again

Darling, promise me you won't try that
Never again

What was it that we were?
Because we weren't together
Not in the sense of people who last forever
But we weren't strangers
Not after the topics we talked about
We were too similar, too close
And at the same time
As different as the stars
Such close proximity
A million miles apart

Whenever I give myself the slightest indulgence
It's like my senses become heightened to the way
My stomach bulges at the top of my jeans
The skin folding over the fabric
The heavy feel of my thighs
Sticks to my chair in the summer
My stomach rolls when I sit
I lean slightly forward to hide it
Instead amplifying the feeling
Of the way my chest is disproportionate from the rest
Of me, like my soul is stuck in a body of a person
I wasn't supposed to be

I've found myself looking at flowers more
I wonder if they bloom because they long to be loved
Or if they bloom because
They're already so loved
They feel the security of knowing love's waiting
They bloom without that fear stunting their growth
They are free; you can see it in every flower
Like I've never known before

My darling, I fall in love easily
And if you're anything like me
I pray you have a gentle heart that mends easy
For we by nature fall in love easy

I'm convinced that I'll never be desired
Not until I lose over twenty pounds
Or grow seven inches taller
I'm starting to find the latter more plausible
Don't make me count the number of diets that I've tried
To squeeze back down to my old size
That I haven't worn since I was fourteen
The body of a person I used to be
In my head, she's all grown up
Perfect and beautiful with visible collar bones
She's muscled and strong and happy
Oh, she's so happy, just look at that brightness in her eyes
It elevates then devastates me
I fear no one will ever know that side of me
Because I don't know if I can still become
The woman I was supposed to be

Did you know once I drove twenty minutes
Just to see a boy
And you know something even funnier
I thought it was love
So don't pity yourself for the choices you made
Falling quickly, I've always been this way

I'll never find enough words to say
How it just felt nice
To be in a boy's car, who could drive well
Who didn't make me fear for my life with every corner
They're dulled now, but I remember the nerves
Scrambled beneath the sweater I wore to hide
Every bone, every curve
I wondered what I was doing, smiled at my feistiness
Feeling like I had tricked an evening from him in a great heist
But he had said yes, and willingly,
Though I didn't understand why someone like him
Would want to go out with me
But I liked it anyway
And welcomed the coming change
Being with him, it felt familiar like I'd found a lost connection
More at home, less of a sojourner
Yet there were things I didn't understand
Why I wanted to be near him but would turn my head
And look out the windshield when I couldn't think
Of anything to say
I kept him just at the edge of the corner of my eye
Where I saw just the shape of his outline
To give me something to mull in my mind
And give color to the pictures that I fabricated
I'm so sorry, but even from the first date
I remember wishing that I would turn my head and
See someone else
Like I didn't trust that he or I were enough for the other
Maybe it was that it felt right to be with someone
I hesitated from the beginning if he was the one
I can tell you that my heart sank under my ribs
When he told me that he didn't care about the outdoor things
And I have a feeling it was right then that he started to doubt
(If he hadn't already been questioning his decision)

For my accent gave it away; it drawls when I get nervous
And he left me struggling for a cool breath
But he—he's not that way
I can't help it
No beating around the bush is ever going to help me better say
That I think too often on when was the exact moment that he
Told himself that I wasn't enough
What parts of me did he pick apart in the conclusion
And say, *She's a great personality but nothing of illusion;*
I've seen more interesting trees or clouds,
Any of the outside things;
She's pale like she hides from the sun;
She looks like she doesn't know that she needs to run,
And lose a few pounds to fit back into that thinner waist.
Was that what made him decide to not wait
For another date to see if I was someone
He could love

Of all the places I've seen
Of all the people on the sidewalks
In the hallways
In my schools
Of all the ones I've given
More of myself than they could handle
Of all the loves I thought I wanted
You were the nicest man I ever met

While I fall quickly, I don't think it's into love
No, I'm certain
If it is love, it's not the kind that lasts
It's the fleeting stuff that rises and vanishes
As quickly as lightning flashes
And just the same in wicked thunderstorms
It rages and it roars
But it doesn't rain forever
And when the clouds glide emptily by
It leaves the damage that I survey
A battleground of brokenhearted scars marking its wake
But does not spring come with showers and storms?
Is it not the sky's tears that make the flowers grow?
On this I shall ponder as I have with every breath
For the last twenty and some years

Funny how the easiest to get over
Was the nicest one to date
Wonder if I'll ever change
Not likely
I'm a woman with stubborn ways

I'm curious if I'll ever see my collarbones again
Right now, they're buried under a person I don't want to be
I let food try to fix me but instead it consumed me
And now I just want to see my collar bones again

The Things I Never Said

There are things I've never said
Not to anyone, not yet
I don't know how they will react
If I talk about the dark things of my past
But these are not universal just to me
These are things I fear will never cease to be
Not in this life, not in this time
I'm not the only girl who struggles with a pack
Of burdens that I wrestle onto my back
And strap across my chest before I'm allowed to start the day

When I saw him, my arms rose to meet him
Even though he stood across the way
Like gravity was weakened by the years that I'd missed him
And it could no longer keep a tight hold on me
He caught me in his arms and held me tight
I didn't worry if my side squished beneath his hand
Or pray he didn't notice that I'd grown bigger
I didn't realize that I wasn't worried
Until the middle of the moment
When I didn't recognize the emotions I felt
Because joy and peace had become such strangers to me
Do you understand what I'm telling you?
That I'm trying to say that it's once in a blue moon
That I feel safe enough to look at someone
Not blood kin to mine own and say, *I love you*
Do you understand what I mean?
I don't know how to give someone else
What I'm still trying to remember how to give to myself

I never said how active
My imagination builds stories
Of the littlest things
When you told me of your siblings
(Remember that night?)
I pictured rowdy boys who felt like family
I pictured a beautiful girl
Familiar to me because y'all share features
And her name sounded sweet
And added to the way I felt like we'd already met
Though I'd never seen the day
I pictured her at my height—sweet and kind
A lot like her brother, pretty smile to turn heads
And I felt like I could see us all as dear friends
It made me want to have a sweet family
And I know it's all hypothetical
But I think I would have really liked yours
A part of me worries that your mother
Would have hated me
For how I dressed, the things I love
And without losing myself
I would've tried to fit in her world
Like, for instance, I thought of brunch
Why thoughts of your family
Made me think of midday breakfast
I can't say
But I could just see us: me, your mother, your sister
Laughing and sipping orange juice
So real, it hurts like a memory
I have to remind myself
It's nothing but a stark daydream

When his name appears at the top of my screen
It takes me a minute
When I forget that we're not anything
Beyond something that used to be
In a moment, like I'm suspended on the tipping point
I balance between forgetting and remembering
In that little moment, I forget to remember
That he broke things off
I forget how to feel
I forget who I'm supposed to be
Suspended, I'm divided by a thin string
From whom I could have been in relation to him
From whom I am today because of him
We could have been more
Had it not ended after one date
When we didn't even walk that far

And then I looked at you as you passed on the sidewalk
And it felt just grand
—like I held in a laugh
Because I no longer shook when I looked at you
It felt like I finally figured out how to remove
Your memory from my hand
And when you asked how I was
I looked at you
And had to ask myself how I ever thought I'd loved you
And it was the best feeling I'd ever held on my lips
It was goodbye, freedom like a kiss

Is this healing?
Is this how it feels?
I'm opening cupboards I haven't touched in years
Looking for gloves, shovels, rakes
There's so much to do
But I'm excited—in a quiet determination kind of way
I'll be in the garden, should anyone need me
I think I'll be alright

She is wild, and I will love her

- *Excerpt from my love letter to myself*

Who would have thought
The day would come
That I'd wish I'd been born of the city
So I could have you back in my life
But I'm not of that world
Give me the mountains
Give me the flowers
Give me the wildest things
For they are free
Dwelling in the places where I feel
Most like me
And I prefer it that way
I'm not of your world
And I can't ask you here to join me

I hoped by now the days of crying in my car would be over
But today proves that's certainly not the case
I'm sitting under the sunroof and fighting back sobs
Because I'm stuck in a memory, staring at your face
Crying, begging internally for you to give me another chance
Thinking how I would change everything I had said
I've realized what I mean is that
I'm saying I could change for you
But we both know that's not fair
Because you deserve someone whom
Will enjoy your games with passivity
A woman uninterested in sports
But is much better versed in looking like yours
I'm not that girl
I could try, but she'll never be me
And I'm not sure if I want to be her
I think this is how healing is supposed to be
Even if it means that I take my walks alone
I'd rather grow old with only the sunshine to hold
Than play the part you'd cast me
Where I'd be perfect in every conceivable way
And I'd play the part like I stood on the stage
For the world was watching
Drawn to your reputation
While I'd be dying with internal petitions
To depart from you if it meant I could, at last,
Be the way God made me

I've lost the words to describe the sunset
Other than that, I want to watch it with someone

I'll be alright over this little matter
I learned so much from what never was
In this little matter, I found within myself
The courage to ask and see
I found my confidence
To take an action that requires more than diligence
I put myself up for speculation
For I know that I am made fearfully, wonderfully
And the God who saves has never abandoned me
He held my hand as I asked
And he held my heart when you thanked me kindly
And gave the invitation back

Staring at the blue veins that run beneath my chest
I think of how strange it is
To be fully functioning as an independent
Yet live crippled in mortal dependency
On my need to fill the absent place of romance in my life
With whomever passes by
One after the other
They come, never stay
I watch another walk away
And it shouldn't hurt so much
When nothing is ever more than a crush
And I never speak
It's always just in my head
The conversation that I wish we'd had
And to where they could have led
But it still hurts
And the blue veins running in my pale chest tell me why

If I am nothing more than a tree
Subject to the seasons
Then I will stretch out my arms for the robins
On which to sit
And bloom in the face of the frost
With a challenge of a grin

Give me a reason to hate you
Let me look at your face
And summon all the courage of the things I have to say
Fully knowing that I forget everything but my name
When you look at me in that open and honest way
You would mourn if you knew
How hung up I am over you
But it's not you and I know it
I know it when I think how I would've had
To walk through a restaurant
Pretending to be more than I am
To justify to society how your arm
Carried the weight of my hand

I'm earthy and wild
And there with him now
Walking in the memory
Walking with him
Coming home from the game
Letting him be alone with the boys
To celebrate another win on the roster
But he insists on first seeing me home
Because he knows that I hate
To kiss him in public
But I don't mind on my doorstep
In the halo-yellow of the little porch light,
And I hug his neck though he says,
I'm pretty sweaty
But hard work doesn't scare me away
I'll want to hug him anyway
Kiss him again on the cheek
And say, *You played great today*
He tells me goodbye one last time
Then leaves me to think of him
The rest of the night

Read what I pen
Every now and then
Until it becomes every night
That you read my work into the late hours
By the faint fight of our bedstand lamplight
To wane off the stars for a few minutes more
Reading line after line
About the day we spent together

The Things I Never Said

The things I never said
Never seem to end
They are the outpouring of who I am
The Guinevere to my Camelot
For it will be my ruin
If I let myself dwell on it much longer
If I never learn to forget what's been forgiven
I'm doomed to my ruin
After six years of this
Shouldn't I have learned how to accept
The girl I was
And the woman I've become
Rather than fall asleep hungry
And stumble through the morning
On into the evening to crush the woman I am
Into my self-idolized sense of perfection
That proves to myself
That I am enough
Or is it that I just need the distraction
Until I forget to compare myself
To the woman across the room
The one sitting next to you
Who looks the way I thought I'd be
Or is it that the only person who needs convincing
That I am enough
Is the woman I see fighting herself in the mirror
Wrestling with who she is
And who she was supposed to be

You're like water that's flooded the spring
I was never meant to be a marsh
Yet you've changed the forest into a swamp
I was meant for Colorado in the fall
Not Florida in the summer rain
You are for the beach
As I am for the mountains
Unless we meet on the cliffs
I fear we are meant to go different ways

I think of you like the soft blanket
In the trunk beneath my bed
And though I know the idea only lives in my head
I wish it were real
I wish that you were here
Soft, warm, heavy
Around my shoulders
Gentle to my body
Protecting my insecurities

If I never find a good one to marry
I'll flirt with his memory
To pass the time and occupy
My mind with hopeless premonitions
Of what I wish could be
My reality instead of the life
I can only find in my dreams
I've never seen it but
I know what it'll look like
Warm sunshine, golden as his eyes
When they catch the light
Before he smiles at me
Darling, I see us dancing
With the windows open in the kitchen
Baking muffins for the weekend
And it will make me thank God for him
All the more
Because I found him
But it can't be real
We're barely friends
It's just a little daydream

All I want is for you to hold my hand
Kiss me on the cheek
And tell me goodnight in the yellow moonlight
Pooled on my front porch

You know that window that I said you make me think of
The big one where I sit to watch the rain
I think it's broken today
The glass has fogged over
Clouding it from a window into a mirror
It's taken my view of torrential skies
Of the wind shredding the trees
As the rain pounds sideways in slants of a downpour
And it's turned it into a picture frame
Of me, sitting on the living room floor
Crying while I'm cutting flowers for a bouquet
That I picked by myself for my kitchen table
Because the place looked like it needed some color
Except now they have me crying in my living room
Because a thorn went through my thumb
Drawing blood, yes, but mostly tears
How many times have I pushed away something good
Because I didn't understand what love was doing for me
How many times have I drawn love's blood
Screaming at it to leave the flowers behind

Thank goodness
For back roads
In the hills of the county
That nobody knows
From the place where everyone asks
How am I supposed to get home
From here, I find no fear
It's peace
Peace in the sound
Of my tires churning dust from the ground
With the radio
As the only friend I know
And the windows down
To listen to the old forgotten sound
Of how it feels to break a heart
And put it back together again

I need to go back to that childhood place
Where the music filled me,
The last place I felt safe
Where the earth made me think
I could be anything
As long as I dreamed

I had a friend who threw a tea party
She didn't know I was still at the wake
Mourning the memory
Of the way you walked away
From me, again, like everyone it seems
Truth be told, I didn't feel much like going
But I dressed up for my own sake
I needed a reason to feel pretty in the worst way
I took my mother's old dress from the back of the closet
And wrapped a sweater over the top
To hide the way the buttons gape and don't close right
To feel something soft to warm my skin
Comfort me in a way not even I can
The black fibers of the sweater clung to the flowered dress
Like even it didn't really feel like going
And I curled the fronts of my hair
Giving me a wild child air
That had been tamed for society's sake
Who'd let them pick the grass from her tangled hair
And run a comb through it until it lost the way it curls
Wild and free
Taken the dirt stains from her play jeans
Washed the mud from her knees
Stripped her dresser of the silly t-shirts
And wrapped her in the cloth that they said
Made her good enough
To sit with them at their table in the cafeteria
Turned something polished out of something perfectly rough
Walking down the sidewalk
I looked like the older version of that little girl
Polished and tight-lipped with a soft, unfeeling smile
The only emotion a rugged dejection
Like a mourner for the loss of the person I used to be
I held that little girl's hand

Who just wanted to be happy and free
And she bit her tears in her lip
The freshly scrubbed skin on her face burning red
For embarrassment at holding such love
In little dirt-stained hands and being told,
You as yourself is not enough
I walked down the sidewalk
With the bag on my shoulder
The one you never saw but I love
A gift from my youngest brother
And I wore my heels that you also never saw
Because we never came close to that road
Of dinner dates and fancy dreams
We were apart 'fore the leather could wear at the seams
I walked into the room, heavy of heart
Afire with scorned rejection
At myself for the way the long dress hung around my hips
I blamed it again as the reason why I'd never felt love's kiss
I hated you that day for sitting next to me in every thought
In every way, like you were there in the chair beside me
Without stepping foot in the room
The party was fine
And once I relaxed, I finally had fun
But no one knows that when I got home
I cried hard that day

Funny how we talked about gardens
And because of you
I bought work gloves with a calico pattern
I'm finally weeding the brambles overgrown in me
I make no predictions for us
But please know that when the little
Yellow flowers sprout
I will thank God for using you
To remove my blindness
From what I need to do

I never asked more about your faith
After your story of how you found your way
There's a lot of things that I don't like to speak of
And faith shouldn't be one of them
But it feels so a part of me
That if I talk about it, it feels like I'm bare
For anyone to see

Love fades
After so many years running away
So now I can only feel it in memory
Like the moon on an overcast night
I know it's behind the clouds
But I can't see the light

He has no idea that
When I see him in the morning
My stomach twists
My chest tightens
Like in the beginning
When it first started to happen
All over again

Welcome to the other side of how I think
Holding the deepest part of myself back
Like pulling a starving horse from drowning itself
In the river while it drinks
I've got the reins in my hand
I could turn left to resign and let go
Ride to the west with a low brim and a fiery sunset
To burn the words out of me that you'll never know
But I could flick the bit to the right
And find an all-out, knock out, dragged down fight
Because self-preservation says to take dignity and run
But curiosity says to take course
With courage and chase the sun
Raise a sail to take the ocean by storm
Catch the breeze till my boots beach on the shore
Of the island of hope
Where the tides pulling me to the idea of you, evermore
Even though I know fully well that we wouldn't work out
But I can't set it down
I've got to carry this pack with my load
Until it falls off my back or I find the end of one of the roads
Because I can't decide which way to go
Which road leads me to the person I call Home
I'm sitting at the crossroads of
Hold onto what's been lost or fully let go
Forgive myself for what I wouldn't change
Not blame you for why we met a short fuse
Fizzled the fire and drowned the dying embers
That now keep my company at the campsite
I make at the crossroads of which way I'm to go
Because no matter which way I chose
There is something I'll lose
To go wears the shoes from my horse's feet
For who knows how far I'll go before I find something

That resembles half of what looks like home
Yet to stay takes my dignity and lays down my pride
Among the dying embers as the fire cries
Because while I whisper words to see if it still holds life
You decide if it lives or dies
If here I stay to build
Or go to follow the pull of the westward tide

I'm tipping on the end of today
And the edge of tomorrow
Suspended like on a wire
Of elation and sorrow
Because I had you to myself
Even for but half a day
And the list is awfully slim
Of those whom I've let take me away
From my little room in my quaint apartment
And I let you take me on some adventure

I think there's a part of me still out there
Driving with him around our sleepy town
Under the stormy, moonlit, dark sky
I'm still sitting next to him
Wondering what I'm supposed to do
I'm still grasping for words to make sense
Of what I need to say to convince him
To give me another chance

I don't dream of him often
But when I do
I wake up in the morning looking for him
Because I have the talent of building up in my head
Us together like a storybook to be read
Of chapters of pages
To be told for generations into the ages
Not something that lasted enough
To be a fraction of a chapter
To tell all of what happened
The subjective material will fit in three pages
The rest would be objective
In all its derivatives and durations
Because for something too shallow to drown
I've given it power like on its head I've set a crown
Not as bad as in the past
But I hope I've learned that lesson at last
And the truth in that is evident
For I'm the one who made this connection relevant
And I'll always wonder if he'd have ever spoken
If I'd have let us be known by name
And the rest of it stay broken
Go back in time and cut the wires
That bound us to meet
Leave destiny bolted outside the door in the street
Because I don't want to regret knowing his face
But I'm sick of finding that he leaves like the rest
Without a trace
Yet, still, he's different than the others
He showed a strong chest

Made it clear he enjoyed the time
Considered himself blessed
Spoke strong and clear, straight to my face
Said maybe in another time, another place

I wish you were here
To hold my hand, to tell me it will all be okay
Because alone here in agony makes me
Acutely aware all over again
Of how it felt when you walked away
No, maybe not to that extreme
For you know I dramatize
And live in my imagined works of make-believe
But there is something to be said for the way I romanticize
Everything that could have been
Had I fought harder to try again
But words now mean little
We're not in process
We're a finalized transaction

What could it hurt to try once more
Take a walk after practice when the sun goes down
Let the lights yellow the shadows
On the sidewalk as we walk through early night
Maybe feel the back of his hand
Brush mine
Once, twice
Then his fingers take mine
Cradle it like something delicate, something new
Like day at first light before the sky turns faint blue

Looking at him
From across the room
I wonder if my head would fit in the cove
Between his chest and neck
Like a stranger coming home
To a well-made bed
A safe place to rest
To weather the storm
As the sea crashes against the rocks of the coast
Safe—for a while
To leave if I must at least with the memory
Of a friendly smile and tender hand
That made my heart glad to know a man
Who understood the sleepy little parts of me
That just needed to rest and gently be
Left alone but cradled in a strong hold
Because I am as volatile as the sea
And the land-locked world misunderstands me
When I say that I want him
What I think I mean is that I want *him*
My only
To be him
And I know that's unfair
But when is life ever fair
What if this is the best that is ever to come
That I've finally found someone to whom I will run
Instead of away, farther and farther away
Until I'm so lost that it's only my voice I hear say,
Where have you gone, child
As I run deeper into the forests that make me grow wild

Well, would you look at that
It is true
God makes art out of broken things

I looked at him like a blank canvas
On which to write the story I want to live
Which isn't fair to him or me
To force something that can't give or receive
The right kind of love
For I think of it as an arm to hold
On the sidewalk, in a crowd, under the stars
I don't know how he thinks
It may be in words
—I would have cheered at his games
Or maybe he thinks in actions
—I'd have had cookies in the oven in five minutes
If it's acts of service that makes him want to stay
I'd have found a way to do it for him
—Even just offering to pick up the next bale of hay
I never told him this
But when I spoke about him with a friend
She asked of his hometown
And exclaimed, *That's an easy drive*
To meet his parents on a weekend
And what was I supposed to do
So hopeless, so desperate
For something to have, something like him
That I fell into the thought
And wondered what life could be like under a big sky's blue
If we had children, which should be implied
For I want plenty
Of seats crowded around my dining room table
If we had children
I know he'd have bought them gloves and balls
And supported them through every ride, every fall
He'd have spent the evenings playing with them
Helping me in the kitchen, scrubbing a casserole pan
And the wind would stir the open window's curtains

Wrapping around the earthy tones of the room
As I dry a dish and he sweeps with a broom
What a facade
To grow teary eyed and vigorously nod
In wishful dreaming for desperate thinking
Of knowing how badly I want the scene
I just don't think the parts were cast for him and me
But I want them to be because he's right there
And I don't want to wait another year
Or two or three or eight as the anticipation scars and sears
The broken bits of my silly domestic dream
Into a mangled trail of rugged abandon
Reduced to but a gleam
Of the dream that it used to be
Because even if we're not perfect
I think a safe home is worth it
A life well spent with a man with strong hands
And a willing heart to change plans
And go on adventures on a whim
Because I don't know if I'll ever find another like him
Even if he's never worn boots for shoes
Even if we contrast like night to day
Even if there's no guarantee we'll ever be more than okay
Because right now, he's right here
And his eyes look like the blue sky—clear

The things I never said
The confessions I utter in my head
Muttering my misfortune
For never taking the opportunity
To give life to my chest
When you leveled your leave in front of me
But I blame your genetics
For the face that looked at me that way
And gave me hope
That I might want someone to stay
These confessions give me nothing
They don't reconcile our decided fate
Yet I voice them in ink as if to measure with tape
The exact distance we've separated
How far we'll go to see each other yet be estranged
For it is in our hands, we hold our destiny
And though, we make it what we work to be
You spoke the truth when you said,
Better as friends, to describe you and me

Apparently now, it's also the weather
That makes me miss you
It's warm after the storm
And all I can think
Is that I want you with your arms around me
I want my head pressed beneath your chin
Tucked right against your chest
Where I can feel your heart beat its steady rhythm
Whispering to mine that you've got me
I'm safe in your arms
I don't know how I've reached this point
Where I associate you with safety
But I'm so far lost in the manifest
Of the storming hue in your eyes
That I can't see the rest of the sky

The Things I Never Said

I never said I liked the brown in your blond
But I do, the way it curls at the ends
It reminds me of something familiar
Something more than friends
I never said a lot of things
Like that, I liked the blue in your eyes
The faint color like morning
Pure, like clear skies unable to shed the rain
No tempest brewing on the horizon in a storm's warning
Not a pressure to run but to hesitate for maybe, just maybe
This shattered shell has found a strong hand to hold
While dancing in the middle of a summer night's kitchen
In a full house in which to live and grow old
I never said a lot of things
Like I never said that I've never held eyes so kind
I never said that I liked the way you played
Music and the way you sang
But it spoke of your character
And made me want to love you more
Eve when I wasn't sure
If what you are is what I wanted
If all of you could be who I needed
Or if I'd have to take you in bite-sized pieces
To swallow the idea of life with a man
So different than me in every conceivable way
Except for a mutual attraction
But even that is speculation
Because I never asked what you thought of me
And what I'll never know still haunts me

Of all the things I never said

Of all the confessions that I've scribbled from my head
Of the all the emotions I've learned to understand
This is the last of the things I'll think of you
And then I'll put away the fret
Know this:
You were the kindest man I ever met

The things I never said to you
The sides of me you'd have slowly discovered
The conversations that would have come later
You'd have learned the way I fight and love
And what I wish to keep covered
You see I feared the day
That I had to decide if I wanted to go or wanted to stay
Because it seems the decision always rests on my shoulders
Yet for once you made the decision
And how it hurt to learn you saw me as more sister or brother
I don't love easily
I give and give, and I pour
And I pour from myself until there is no more

After all the years
After all the losses, all the repetitions of time
Of climbing mountains of hope
To slide to the ground and pour my wounds into rhymes
I'm not sure what it's supposed to look like
If it will catch me off guard from the front or behind
If I should keep looking in the flatlands
Or find a mountain to climb
Because I've spent every day looking so hard, I've gone blind
To the goodness that can exist
In the soul of a man's chest
My expectations are broken and cold
Because in these small boys, I find no rest
Not a hug to hold me when my head grows heavy
Not a compliment to fill my eyes with a new kind of tears
Not a story to make me laugh or sweetly pass the time
Not a one with whom to grow old and spend the years
And I know I've jumped to drastic conclusions
Coming up with these far-off dreams
But at least I stick to tradition
Because he's not the first for whom I've wondered
And not the first for whom I've put pen to paper
But he's the first in many ways
I've never wanted something to be so real
Thank him for me for the adventure
For it reminded me of what I want to call home
A quiet place, in the mountains, a place
Of little domestic things

I think one of the hardest parts
Of growing up
Is learning what to let go of
And what to pull close

About the Author

An Arkansas native, K.L. Neal is an upcoming author and poet, who loves good stories, livestock, and a well-made pair of blue jeans. *The Things I Never Said* is her first self-published work.

You can stay up to date with her upcoming books on Instagram at @klnealauthor.

Author Acknowledgements

Despite the years I have carried this dream, I could not have done this without the continuous love and support of my dear, wonderful mother. In addition, the support of my family continues to overwhelm me. To each of you, thank you for teaching me the power of stories. We'll see if I can learn to captivate a crowd like Dad.

Many friends peers and colleagues also continuously offered advice and listened to me drone on about my ideas and hopes and dreams. Thank you all for your patience and feedback.

Thank you, also, to my readers! Here's to the start of a grand adventure.

Thank you, Lord, for giving us hearts to dream big.

Made in the USA
Columbia, SC
03 August 2023

21216066R00088